CLASSICAL SOLOS FOR F HORN

VOLUME 2

ONLINE MEDIA INCLUDED
Audio Recordings
Printable Piano Accompaniments

PLAYBACK+
Speed • Pitch • Balance • Loop

To access recordings and PDF accompaniments, visit:
www.halleonard.com/mylibrary

Enter Code
2311-3278-3811-8249

ISBN 978-1-70516-755-7

Visit Hal Leonard Online at
www.halleonard.com

World headquarters, contact:
Hal Leonard
7777 West Bluemound Road
Milwaukee, WI 53213
Email: info@halleonard.com

In Europe, contact:
Hal Leonard Europe Limited
1 Red Place
London, W1K 6PL
Email: info@halleonardeurope.com

In Australia, contact:
Hal Leonard Australia Pty. Ltd.
4 Lentara Court
Cheltenham, Victoria, 3192 Australia
Email: info@halleonard.com.au

LARGO
from *Xerxes*

F HORN

GEORGE FRIDERIC HANDEL
Arranged by PHILIP SPARKE

00870108

SONGS MY MOTHER TAUGHT ME

from *Gypsy Songs*

ANTONÍN DVORÁK
Arranged by PHILIP SPARKE

F HORN

MINUET NO. 2
from *Notebook for Anna Magdalena Bach*

F HORN

Attributed to CHRISTIAN PEZOLD
Arranged by PHILIP SPARKE

LA CINQUANTAINE
from *Two Pieces for Cello and Piano*

JEAN GABRIEL-MARIE
Arranged by PHILIP SPARKE

F HORN

00870108

6

SEE, THE CONQUERING HERO COMES

from *Judas Maccabeus*

GEORGE FRIDERIC HANDEL
Arranged by PHILIP SPARKE

F HORN

00870108

SONATINA
Op. 36, No. 1

MUZIO CLEMENTI
Arranged by PHILIP SPARKE

F HORN

SERENATA

from *String Quartet, Op. 3, No. 5*

F HORN

FRANZ JOSEPH HAYDN
Arranged by PHILIP SPARKE

Andante cantabile (♩ = 96)

TAMBOURIN
from *Second Suite in E Minor*

JEAN-PHILIPPE RAMEAU
Arranged by PHILIP SPARKE

F HORN

00870108

WALTZ
from *Album for the Young*

PYOTR ILYICH TCHAIKOVSKY
Arranged by PHILIP SPARKE

F HORN

SONATINA
from *Six Pieces, Op. 3*

CARL MARIA VON WEBER
Arranged by PHILIP SPARKE

F HORN

Moderato e con amore
(♩ = 120)

GAVOTTE
from *Paride ed Elena*

CHRISTOPH GLUCK/arr. JOHANNES BRAHMS
Arranged by PHILIP SPARKE

F HORN

Grazioso (♩ = 72)

00870108

SONATA
Op. 118, No. 1

ROBERT SCHUMANN
Arranged by PHILIP SPARKE

F HORN

00870108

SERENADE

from *Schwanengesang, D.957*

F HORN

FRANZ SCHUBERT
Arranged by PHILIP SPARKE

Andante con moto
(♩ = 84)

SONATINA
Anh. 5, No. 1

LUDWIG VAN BEETHOVEN
Arranged by PHILIP SPARKE

F HORN

Moderato
(♩ = 126)

00870108

BOURRÉE
from *Flute Sonata, HWV 363b*

F HORN

GEORGE FRIDERIC HANDEL
Arranged by PHILIP SPARKE

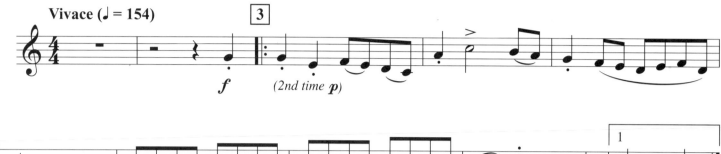

00870108